For Finlay, Jamie, and Dad with love.
—S.W.

Illustrations © 2004 Sue Williams
© 2004 Standard Publishing, Cincinnati, Ohio. A division of
Standex International Corporation. All rights reserved. Sprout logo
and Music to See™ are trademarks of Standard Publishing.
Printed in Italy.

Concept: Diane Stortz.
Project editor: Lindsay Black
Cover and interior design: Suzanne Jacobson.

ISBN 0-7847-1512-2

11 10 09 08 07 06 05 04   9 8 7 6 5 4 3 2 1

Yes, Jesus Loves Me

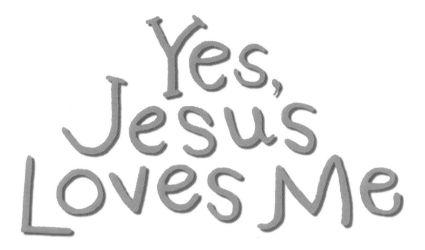

illustrated by

Sue Williams

STANDARD PUBLISHING

CINCINNATI, OHIO

Jesus loves me, this I know,

For the Bible tells me so.

He's got the whole world in his hands.

Little ones to him belong.

They are weak, but he is strong.

He's got the whole world in his hands.

Yes, Jesus loves me!

Yes, Jesus loves me!

Yes, Jesus loves me!

He's got the whole world in his hands.

He's got the wind and the rain
in his hands.

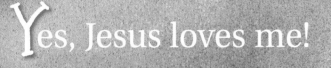
Yes, Jesus loves me!

He's got the little bitty baby
in his hands.

Yes, Jesus loves me!

He's got you and me brother, in his hands.

He's got you and me sister, in his hands.

He's got e-v-erybody here
in his hands.

He's got the whole world in his hands.

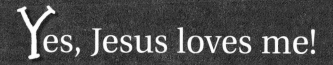

Yes, Jesus loves me!

Yes, Jesus loves me!

Yes, Jesus loves me! . . .

He's got the whole world in his hands.

Jesus Loves Me

Anna B. Warner

He's Got the Whole World in His Hands

Traditional Spiritual

He's got the whole world_____ in his hands.__ He's got the

whole wide world,_____ in his hands.__ He's got the whole world_____

in his hands.__ He's got the whole world in his_____ hands.